PJ's, Pearls, & Fishing Poles

Life Lessons of Style & Substance

By
Penny Davis

Who they were is who we are.

There wasn't one specific moment that I decided to write this book but more a collection of remarkable Hospice stories that very much needed to be shared.

Although this book honors the patients, families and the Hospice Interdisciplinary Team (better known as the IDT) for their caring and dedication, the central theme is the importance of time and life lessons. Although Hospice is the final stage of an individual's life journey, this book is neither focused on death nor on the dying process. This is a book about how to live until the end of our lives with meaning. The individuals on these pages offer extraordinary life lessons, which serve as a legacy for all of us.

Choosing Hospice isn't about giving up but the heart and soul of living. If we're open to the world around us, we can learn a lesson from everyone every day in some way. The patients and their families introduced in these pages prove that truth. Woven into their stories are examples of deep and abiding love, wisdom, humor, traditions, honor, friendships, resilience, zest, courage, respect, generosity, spirit, compassion, pride.............. and I am just the messenger.

PJ's, Pearls, & Fishing Poles

First published by Dog Ear Publishing
4010 W. 86th Street, Ste H
Indianapolis, IN 46268
www.dogearpublishing.net

ISBN: 978-1-4575-2326-7

This book is printed on acid-free paper.

Printed in the United States of America

Dedication

As always, family comes first
To Rod, Becky, Rachel, Regan, Rylee, Trey
& Ryan, Jolie, Tanner, Blake, Ethan.
You are the smile on my face
and the love in my heart.

To Interdisciplinary Teams
(IDT's) everywhere.
You are truly heroes every single day.
You give strength, guidance, peace and love
To the patients and their families
which is an extraordinary gift.

Prologue

For me it probably all began as a little girl helping my Grandmother care for an ailing neighbor throughout one long hot summer. My job was to carry oatmeal in the morning and soup at lunch as carefully as I could down the sidewalk without spilling a drop.

My Grandmother's neighbor and dear friend lived on a corner of Grandmother's street, and that summer she was very ill. All of her friends formed a schedule to meet her needs. Food was the assignment for Grandmother and me. Others gave baths, read books to her, kept her home tidy, or provided bouquets. I remember that a vase of colorful, fragrant fresh cut flowers always sat on her bedside table. I have no idea how far into the past is rooted the ritual of providing flowers when people are ill, but it dates at least to medieval days, when physicians suggested that flowers' fragrances would displace the "bad air" and bring healing properties. The ritual is as meaningful today as it was many centuries ago.

Our childhood experiences help shape our futures in intriguing ways. Grandmother's network of friends provided Hospice services decades before Hospice was recognized as a level of care. I am a forty-five-year career veteran in health care. I've walked the halls of hospitals giving care. I have directed Hospice programs on site. And, I have traveled the highways managing multiple Hospice programs as an Area Vice President. Of all my job titles, my favorite is Executive Director, where I work with a team to manage a program of care for patients facing the end of their lives. I cannot think of a more rewarding career. It touches everyone involved, both personally and professionally.

According to Hillary Clinton, "It takes a village" to raise a child and in the world of Hospice " It takes a team " to provide the very best care.

Chapter 1

The Interdisciplinary Team

I live in the Midwest, where the month of August is always hot and humid. The swirling dirt at the ball park sticks to small players, as well as to the rest of us. On one particular day, several members of our Interdisciplinary Team (IDT) are seated in rows on old wooden bleachers, eating hot dogs dripping with mustard while trying to block out the screams and yells of parents and umpires so we can concentrate on the players fielding the play. A group of ten-year-olds is about to win their baseball tournament.

This is just one place where children learn the art of teamwork and commitment—lessons that will carry them through adulthood. Our Social Worker's son is on the team, and we are his cheering squad on this hot and dusty afternoon. Today we are a team at play. Every day, we are a team at work. But, I'm getting ahead of myself......

Our Hospice office is a modern structure of stone and glass located in a massive complex of office buildings that can only be described as representatives of contemporary architecture. However, we are steeped in traditions, Old World charm, and chocolate.

On a routine Wednesday morning in the middle of the summer, our team gathers around the huge conference room table for our weekly IDT meeting. Here we'll discuss fifty or more patients currently on our Hospice service—which represents half the total number of patients we supervise. The oak table is well worn, littered with bottomless coffee cups, files, patient charts, and stacks of papers needing signatures from various team members. In the center of the table sit two big clear glass cookie jars.

The walls of the conference room are lined with corkboards and chalkboards. This room is the hub of activity and inspiration for our team.

If you glance to the left, you'll see the list of patients who will be visited today by members of the Hospice Interdisciplinary Team, or IDT, as well as a list of new referrals for evaluation, a list of new admissions to add to our service, and special events.

A board to the right is covered with "hands" upon which important messages are written. A simple tracing of a hand is cut from yellow construction paper, representing a "pat on the back" from one team member to another. We display these "pats" for everyone to read. As the Executive Director of our team, I started this practice with high hopes, and the results have become a very important means of recognition among team members. Mark Twain once wrote, "I can live two months on a good compliment." We can, too.

A third board holds an assortment of notes, letters, and thank-you cards from families within our Hospice network. You'll see numerous pictures of our patients interacting with IDT members. The common theme is heartfelt gratitude. Again and again we read comments such as, "We couldn't have gotten through this without you" directed to our team. These notes—not the facts, figures, and statistics—become the measuring stick of our success. They tell us how well we do our job.

One cookie jar contains delicious thick chocolate chip cookies. They will be devoured by the end of the meeting. The other jar contains small pink note cards on which I have written memorable quotes, some from me, others from famous people. These are crucial life lessons that I want to share, short messages borrowed from readings, and inspirational quotes. We start our meeting by randomly drawing out one card. That message will provide our meeting's focus and get us ready for business.

Our IDT is composed of our Medical Director, Nurses, Home Health Aides (HHA), Social Workers, Chaplain, Bereavement Coordinator, Volunteer Coordinator, Sales Team, and myself. We function as a team because we are all committed to quality end-of-life care.

Hospice is a patient-centered approach. Some patients need all the team members at one time or another, while others may require only one discipline. Often patients come to us very late in the life cycle, but in many cases we have weeks or even months to interact with the patient and his or her family. We actually become their extended family. The "cookie cutter" approach never works as well as a program tailored to each situation because all patients and their families have very different needs. Our team members become guests in the patients' and family members' homes—whether those homes are mansions or modest accommodations. What remains the same, however, is our devotion as caregivers.

Our IDT offers pain management, symptom control, comfort, caring, and compassion as we help each patient and family through this poignant time. They offer us invaluable life lessons. Together, as a compassionate team, we become Hospice.

From the cookie jar

"Build Team Spirit"

Coach Vince Lombardi of the Green Bay Packers

Chapter 2

Emily

If ever a woman represented the epitome of a Southern Belle, it is Emily, despite the fact that her husband's job has planted her firmly in the Midwest. Emily embodies all the best Southern values. She and her daughter Elizabeth own an adorable home-decorating shop aptly named " Sophie's Shop," to honor Emily's five-year-old granddaughter Sophie. The shop is small in size, but overflowing in personality, new merchandise, and heirloom pieces. "Sophie's" offers quality items that perfectly blend old and new, tradition and elegance, for many homes— and those items are sent off with generations of Southern advice offered by this mother-and-daughter team.

Once a week I look forward to spending a few hours with a member of our team, visiting patients and their families. We start with a stop at Starbucks for coffee, tea, hot chocolate, or a cool smoothie; the choices depend on the weather. This is my treat as we start our "windshield time" together. I love this opportunity to spend time out of the office with special caregivers, and to witness first-hand our team members commitment. I get to know them better out in their work world.

These dedicated team members drive for miles to see patients, sometimes in the stifling heat of summer, and other times in the deep chill of winter as we drive tentatively over ice-covered roads. Occasionally we choose a perfect summer day bursting with colors and fresh with cool breezes, but our team ventures outdoors in every weather condition imaginable. And they never complain. We all understand the critical importance of their work.

I meet Emily one sunny morning when I am traveling with Nurse on her patient route. We stop in front of a pretty two-story home with a lovely wrap-around porch. This very Southern style home rolls out the welcome mat as soon as we park the car. Rocking chairs and pots of bright red geraniums fill the porch. An American flag is flying in the breeze.

As we approach the front door, we are greeted by a charming lady nestled on a bright green cushion on the gently swaying porch swing. We return her greeting as we step onto the porch. She is dressed in pale pink pajamas and she wears a lovely long string of pearls around her neck as she sips a fruit smoothie. Clearly she is ill, but she looks very peaceful.

Emily notices that I am taking in all the details, and she says simply, "I might be sick and living in my pajamas now, but I will certainly wear my pearls!" I return her smile and hug her. That is when I notice a small beaded evening bag on her wrist. I'm intrigued, but I don't comment.

We help Emily inside her home and settle her in the living room. Nurse begins her visit with lots of questions and comments as she takes notes. Emily discusses the return of breast cancer and what is being done to control the nausea and pain. As she reviews these clinical details, I notice the frequent mentions of her "Nana's Book."

Because I want to give Nurse and Emily some privacy during the examination, I wander into the kitchen and meet Emily's husband Hal, her grand-daughter Sophie, and her daughter Elizabeth. Sophie is an adorable little girl with blond hair, which on this day is pulled back into two pony tails and tied with bright blue ribbons. A bundle of energy, I can tell that she keeps the home lively. We sit at the table drinking sweet tea and discussing all kinds of subjects. Elizabeth reveals that her mother very much wants to leave Sophie a collection of the "Southern Culture Rules" she has accumulated throughout her life. As I listen, I hear about the pieces of information that will be incorporated into the story of "Nana's Book."

Hal smiles at the idea of this legacy his wife plans to leave, and he says how much he appreciates that fact that the women in his life are on a writing mission. It is evident that he adores all three women and he is coping. They are all living with the chal-lenge that breast cancer has presented.

This wonderful family had been shaken by Emily's diagnosis, but they are firm in their belief that life revolves around faith, family and friends. I have found that we all organize our lives in a way that seems optimal for us, but when illness shocks people into a new reality, they need new ways of handling their altered lives. Often the Hospice team is the best solution.

Emily enters the kitchen, and I learn more about "Nana's Book." Our Volunteer Coordinator had assigned a Volunteer to help Emily with her project, and they are having fun assembling the book. Emily explains, " Elizabeth knows all of these bits of wisdom, but I want them to come from me to Sophie. I think it will mean more."

As a grandmother myself, I totally understand. I watch Emily's face light up as she shares details about her plan. It gives her a strong purpose and a focus for Sophie. We speak for a few more minutes. I mention that one of the gifts Hospice offers is the time to undertake meaningful projects like this one because she can remain in her own home.

Over the next several weeks, Emily and her family utilize all of our IDT services, although perhaps the most comforting is the assistance offered by Nurse, whose primary goal is to keep Emily comfortable. Emily very much looks forward to visits from her Volunteer, who reports back to our team about the valuable lessons Emily is teaching her through the book.

As team we have helped patients and families create all types of memory books. But, this is the book that Emily wanted to share and a few lessons she is leaving to Sophie.

" NANA'S BOOK "

Always send a handwritten thank-you note, not an e-mail.

Keep your fingernails filed and polished at all times.

Wear one good piece of jewelry every day.

Keep one pretty lace handkerchief for weddings and funerals

Use cloth napkins for special events and holiday dinners.

Never settle for anything less than a great haircut.

Use baking soda and mayonnaise to remove water rings on wood furniture.

Always have a fresh coat of paint on your front door.

Moisturize your face every day.

Peach cobbler and sweet tea should be on the menu every summer day.

Never put a tomato in the refrigerator. Keep it at room temperature.

A front porch with a swing and potted flowers is a must.

Mix 1/2 cup vinegar with 2 tablespoons baking soda to polish silver.

Our Volunteer also reports that Emily is never seen without her pearls and we still don't know what she keeps in the beaded evening bag.

From the cookie jar

"Having time to meet your goals is invaluable.

We are fully engaged to help."

Chapter 3

Gary

Gary and Connie are the kind of neighbors you find in small towns all around the country. Hardworking, innovative, and dedicated to each other, they entered their sixties with plans to begin enjoying retirement in a few years. Gary had been a pharmaceutical salesman covering an extensive route, and he was more than ready to leave the highway and follow some intriguing side roads for a change. He and Connie had made their plans.

Never in a million years did he think that his fatigue was anything more than the need to slow down. However, Connie was very much the devoted wife and an astute observer. She didn't feel comfortable with what she was seeing, and she encouraged her husband to make an appointment for a physical. The diagnosis of lung cancer was shocking. Because subsequent and extensive treatment failed to change his condition into remission, Nurse and I find ourselves in their home as regular guests, helping them weave the Hospice process into their daily lives.

As we approach the home, Nurse tells me that Gary is a real "take charge type of guy," that he is determined to leave Connie with the knowledge and self-confidence she needs to manage their home and her small business. Because the couple never had children, they have always worked together as a team, depending only on each other for their needs or direction. Throughout their marriage, Gary's job has included writing all checks, ensuring that their home and cars are in good repair, keeping meticulous records, and maintaining a tight ship. Gary, in fact, is beyond organized, I learn during my visit.

As his illness progresses, his primary concern is not his own health, but preparations to make sure that Connie won't become frightened by all her new responsibilities. He is frustrated that their life plans have changed so dramatically—as anyone would be. He is spending his available time documenting directions for everything Connie will need to know and take on.

When we ring the bell at their home, we are greeted by a big shaggy dog named Buddy, and by Connie, who is wearing funky green glasses. We find Gary in the kitchen, a homey room that obviously serves as the center of their daily activities. An old diner booth with a Formica table top and vinyl seats sits in the corner. Gary is there, wearing comfortable sweatpants, a tee-shirt, and a baseball cap on backwards. Papers are spread in front of him on the table.

I introduce myself while Nurse slides into the booth across from Gary to start her visit and discuss how he is feeling. Gary tells her he needs more, or different, pain medications and he is increasingly finding himself short of breath. Nurse makes plans to order oxygen. "My appetite has decreased," he says, "even though Connie has tried to cook and bake everything she can think of for me."

A loyal watchdog, Buddy paces between Connie and Gary. It is apparent that Buddy is an adored and integral part of this small family. "Lie down, Buddy," his two owners say at precisely the same moment. And when that happens, they smile at each other. They are in tune.

Connie is baking something wonderful, I know, sniffing the aromas wafting through the kitchen. I learn that she and her best friend Margo run a small bakery shop called Sweeties, and that the business is a huge success. Open from six o'clock in the morning until three o'clock in the afternoon every day, Sweeties sells cookies, cupcakes, pies, scones, cakes, and breads, as well as their specialty which is cinnamon rolls.

I join Nurse and Gary at the booth, and Connie offers me coffee and a cinnamon roll with thick vanilla icing. It smells heavenly and tastes just as good. I notice the old well worn booth has a coin-operated jukebox, which I admire. Once again I see the special smile pass between Gary and Connie. I marvel at their perfect understanding of each other. As the visit progresses, I learn that traditions play a strong role in their lives together, among them pancakes on Saturday mornings while reading the newspaper and listening to old hit tunes playing on the jukebox.

We chat a few minutes. "How are we doing?" I ask Gary. "Are we meeting your needs?"

He says he has everything he needs, thanks to Connie, Nurse, and our Social Worker. "But can you explain again about the services of your Bereavement Coordinator?"

"We follow families for one year after we no longer care for the patient," I tell him, explaining that we help with the grief process in a variety of ways: through individual meetings as needed as well as support groups on a monthly basis. Gary thinks about what I say for a few minutes. Before we leave, he asks to meet our Bereavement Coordinator. He has decided that is what he wants for Connie.

I ask Gary if he needs any help with the paperwork I see in front of him. Since Gary is not yet of Medicare age, I wonder if he was struggling with insurance papers. But that is not the case, he assures me. "My best friend Charlie will be arriving soon to help with all this," he says. Charlie is the husband of Connie's business partner, he adds. Gary smiles. "The ladies bake, and the guys keep track of the business side of the bakery."

As if on command, the back door opens and a big guy enters without knocking. Gary and Charlie tell me they have been friends since grade school, but I notice that Charlie appears nervous as he claps Gary on the shoulder in greeting. I recognize the problem and slip Charlie a business card as we prepare to leave.

The following day Charlie comes to our office to meet with me. He is embarrassed, he says, because after all the years he and Gary have been best friends, he now doesn't know how to talk to him.

I offer Charlie coffee and a chocolate chip cookie in the conference room, where we chat. I ask him to tell me a few funny stories about their friendship. That request breaks the ice. He recalls hilarious stories of youthful pranks, high school sports, their college days, beer, girls and being each other's best man in their weddings.

Then I point out, "That man is still Gary, and you are still Charlie. Yes, it is a different version of Gary, but you both need each other now more than ever." I give Charlie the same advice I tell everyone who is close to a Hospice patient: "Treat him the same. Remember what you mean to each other. And be sure to talk to him, not at him."

Relief spreads across Charlie's face. He tells me what I already sense: "Gary knows that I will be Connie's support system, and I will be absolutely sure she is safe."

I smile. "Of course you will! That's what best friends do."

The Hospice team knows that often best friends are as close as family. Our Bereavement Coordinator will reach out also to Charlie and Margo and help them cope with the changes that are becoming apparent in Gary's life so they can all support Connie.

From the cookie jar

" *Take the time to stop, look and listen. Then, do what you know is right but not always the easiest thing to do.* "

Chapter 4

Eva

E va and Fred are an adorable elderly couple—there is no other way to describe them. They live in a cluster of small cottages within a retirement village. As the lane winds back to their cottage, I see a curtain pulled to the side of the front window and an elderly man peeking out.

Fred has the door open before we reach the porch. It is apparent that he has been waiting eagerly for this visit. We enter the tidy living room, where a hospital bed sits on center stage. There we find Eva, a tiny, immaculate lady wearing a pale yellow flowered nightgown. Her snow-white hair is clean and combed. The sheets are carefully pulled around her. Fred beams. He is so proud of his wife.

I shake his hand tell him how pleased I am to meet him. He smiles and says, "Eva will be so sorry that she missed you, but this is her naptime." I exchange glances with our Social Worker, who has already informed me that Eva is no longer alert and sleeps all the time.

As we approach the bed, Fred tenderly clasps Eva's hand. I notice the worn thin gold wedding band on her ring finger. He turns to us, smiles, and says, "My bride is just beautiful, isn't she?" And then he winks at her. My heart melts.

I look around the room as Fred and I get to know each other. I notice two chairs sitting around a table that has a chess set on top—and the game is in play. Fred nods and tells me his pals come by each day to play with him. He adds proudly that their wives and the folks from his church keep him in food. I laugh and ask, "Just how many casseroles do you have?"—the standard joke those of us in Hospice all share.

Our Social Worker asks Fred if he has everything he needs. "I do, and I'm so appreciative," he tells us. "All of Eva's needs are being met. The Home Health Aides come to bathe Eva. The Nurses keep her comfortable. The Chaplain visits frequently. And I have friends who come in the evenings so I can take naps."

We return to Eva and once again we see Fred take his wife's hand lovingly. "We have had a happy life," he tells us, and he begins to describe their family.

Everyone has a story to tell and we love his.

Fred and Eva have six daughters who all live in other cities—and, in some cases, other states, he explains. He tells us funny stories about their childhood years, when they were little girls in pigtails and ballet shoes. As the stories progress, he describes how nervous he was as he walked each of his six girls down the aisle and relinquished their hands to the new men in their lives. Since that time, the family has been blessed with grandchildren, who loved to visit Fred and Eva's big old home, where their girls were raised, he says. He then explains how the family home became too much work to maintain and the couple needed to make plans for the future. Fred starts to laugh.

"Want to share ?" I ask.

Fred nods and recalls that when he and Eva decided to downsize and move to this retirement cottage, they offered the grandchildren anything they wanted for their first apartments. "It wasn't much," he says, "but they swarmed over everything with glee, especially the grandgirls. Who knew that our shabby would become something popular, something the girls called 'shabby chic!'" He shakes his head. "Funny how time passes and makes us look at old things in new ways."

The daughters and the grandchildren call frequently, Fred says, telling us that he puts the phone to Eva's ear so they can speak to her. He pauses and leans over to his wife, whispering something in her ear. Then he kisses her cheek. I tell him what he must know: that hearing is the last of our senses to leave us, so he should be sure to keep talking to his wife.

I have no doubt that Fred will. After all, they have been talking to each other for more than sixty years.

Outside the window, Fred has placed a bird feeder, and the winged visitors chirp and sing loud enough to be heard within this peaceful room. I tell Fred again what a great job he is doing as Eva's caregiver, and I remind him that if he needs anything, he is welcome to call the office day or night. "I always mention that we have an answering service that will help you or connect you with someone who can," I say. Sometimes in a moment of need, caretakers may panic and call 911. If an ambulance responds, the emergency medical technicians may transport the patient to a hospital emergency room, and when they are in Hospice, that is no longer the goal.

Early in the morning a few days after my visit with Fred, my first call is from the answering service. The caller says in a chuckle, "You won't believe the call I got from Fred at three o'clock in the morning."

I take a deep breath. "Oh no, what happened? "

Well, it seems that Fred was awake and thinking about the old days. Eva had always made him egg salad sandwiches for his lunch bucket, and he was thinking about that part of his life, which caused him to crave an egg salad sandwich. So, he called the answering service and explained, "I was told that I can call if I need anything. Well, I need to know how to make egg salad." Of course, Fred's request made the night memorable for our answering service. She explained how to boil eggs until they were ready, how to peel them, and then how to make a winning egg salad, with mayonnaise, onion, and celery. Amazingly, thanks to provisions provided by his friends, he actually had all those ingredients in the refrigerator.

At three o'clock in the morning, Fred made himself a special snack. Of course, this is a favorite story for our team.

From the cookie jar

"An act of kindness—no matter how small—can be the most important part of a person's day—for the giver as well as the recipient."

Chapter 5

Danielle

When I introduced myself to Danielle—Dani to her friends—she said something I'll never forget: "Best friends let you rant and rave over the inequities of it all."

Just as quickly, I responded, "And that is why they are your best friends."

Dani smiled back at me and admitted, " Being sick wasn't on my bucket list."

I know. It never is. I hugged her for a long time.

At the age of forty-nine, Dani was told that she had advanced ovarian cancer. Until her diagnosis, she had been teaching third grade in a school where friendships are cherished. She has a host of teacher friends who continue to talk with Dani daily. They keep her "in the loop," so she still feels connected to her previous life. And there are others in the loop. Her husband Evan is a principal at the middle school, and Evan and Dani have a daughter named Natalie, who has just gotten married.

Dani tells me all this as I try not to stare at her blond wig with a bright purple stripe running across it.

As Nurse starts her visit, I walk onto the porch to give them privacy. I am aware that they need to discuss another pain management protocol. Once again I marvel at the Nurses on the IDT, at how talented they are, how they can quickly and surely identify problems, discuss solutions clearly and fully with the Medical Director, and reach quick resolutions. They know, and I know, that our paramount goal is to keep our patients comfortable.

We hear a car arrive. Our Social Worker yells "Hello!" as she comes to the door. "I'm just dropping off goodies for Dani," she says, grinning. I sense a mystery. She tells me she visited Dani yesterday. "We're in cahoots to surprise Natalie, who lives in another state now," she says, adding that a Volunteer is also involved.

I can't wait to hear this story.

Dani is the brains behind the plan. Our Social Worker had been running the errands, but her schedule is so busy that she has called on the services of a special Volunteer. Dani wants to have gifts prepared and wrapped for her daughter, gifts that she will receive every month for a year after Dani is gone. I think to myself, what a sweet idea. I'm anxious to hear the rest of the story because it clearly has them giddy with excitement.

Like all exceptional grade school teachers, Dani has closets full to overflowing with decorations for every season. Every August since she was very young, Nat spent weeks helping her mother prepare her classroom. "Nat is a master at making the room colorful and lively," Dani says proudly. "We also had a tradition of working together to decorate our home for every season."

Dani plans to send Nat a present for her own new home each month, but now she needs helpers to complete the project. I am awestruck as she talks on and on about various ideas. Snowmen salt and pepper shakers for January. Garden gloves and seed packets for May. An album of Nat's baby pictures for October, to help Nat celebrate her birthday. A dozen pretty glass balls for her first Christmas tree in December. Suddenly, everyone is suggesting ideas.

Another yellow hand on the board for our team!

Dani says she wants the gifts put into individual little bags marked by the month. This gives her control. I can't think of anything more special than this flurry of gifts of love from a mother to a daughter. Evan's job will be to mail them each month. This is another way for the father and daughter to stay close and share a tribute from Dani. We are determined to help them achieve their goal.

However, when Dani needs to talk about her health, her worries, and her concerns, she turns to our Social Worker, who is a great listener. We know that many times topics that are difficult to share with close friends and family members can be discussed with our Social Worker or Chaplain. Everyone who faces a terminal illness experiences hard times now and then. We reassure them that they are entitled to express anger and frustration.

Before my visit ends, our Volunteer visits Dani's home. The moment she walks into the house, she stops in her tracks and says, " WOW! Well, WOW! Your wig has a purple streak!"

" Isn't it a hoot? " Dani says with a grin. "My HHA was here this morning, and she outdid herself. She helped me with my bath, adding the lavender bath salts that my teacher friends brought me. Then, in the spirit of lavender, the HHA dyed a streak of purple on my wig because told her I needed to add some color to my life. Remember, I'm used to a room of charming but loud kids and colorful construction paper projects everywhere."

When the Volunteer asked how they managed to find purple dye, Dani told her that the HHA used her creativity: she combined a cream rinse with dry jello. "It will wash out," Dani says confidently, adding, "As my HHA was saying goodbye, she left me a coloring book and crayons as a joke. Thank heavens she has spirit. I needed it."

Thoughtful little activities help lift a patient's gloom and make all the difference.

Nurse tells her, "I am happy you are so happy this morning!" She understands that Dani has a mission.

The disease is progressing, but she is digging deep into her soul to finish her project for Natalie.

As we prepare to leave, I notice a banner of construction paper with glued macaroni and glitter that has been strung across the living room mantle. The macaroni letters spell out a precious message: FEEL BETTER AND WE MISS YOU. The names of Dani's students appear along the border, printed in childish handwriting. Her class is still with her.

It is impossible to express the power of strong friends, upbeat messages, and sympathetic helpers.

We leave Dani dressed in fresh yellow pajamas and her purple striped wig, curled in the corner of the sofa comfortably. Her symptoms are controlled at the moment. "I'm going to be thinking about what to give Natalie for the month of April," she tells us as we say goodbye.

From the cookie jar

"Change is usually difficult, sometimes frightening, but without a doubt change is possible."

Chapter 6

Hank

"The Judge," as we call him, is a ninety-two-year-old lawyer who has served his community as a judge for many years. His face is full of character. On our first visit, we learn that he is the oldest of five generations of Hanks. The youngest is his great-great-grandson, who is five weeks old and affectionately nicknamed "Five." It is immediately apparent that "The Judge" has given much more than his name to the generations in his family.

The Judge now presides over a new courtroom—his living room turned bedroom. Our IDT team adores him and he "holds court" with us frequently, regaling us with courtroom stories that carry invaluable life lessons. He is warm, funny, witty and enjoys talks about "new age" and "old age" practices. As his stories unfold, we learn that his professional passion focused on teens and young adults, educating them about the hazards of drugs, alcohol, and driving.

Late on this particular afternoon, I am riding with our Chaplain on his rounds. We immediately notice that The Judge is weak, but very alert. The team knows how to initiate his plan of care, but we leave him in charge of as many details as possible. He likes structure and order, in his day and in his life. Allowing him to retain a sense of control makes his life more manageable.

Hank plans with precise instructions what time team members should arrive and what they should do for him. True to his calling, he has chosen to use a gavel to alert caregivers of his needs rather than a bell or a shout. When he needs something, he pounds his gavel on the over bed table. We grin at his approach to the bench and we marvel at how unique every patient is.

On this afternoon, the Judge is about to meet his new great-great-grandson for the first time. A five-generation photograph has been planned to celebrate the family's milestone. Five generations, all named Hank, will share a very special family moment. Our HHA has just departed, after readying The Judge for the occasion: fresh pajamas, his thin white hair slicked back, big smile on his face.

The Chaplain and I meet all of the Hanks as they arrive. Just before the photo is taken, The Judge's son Hank helps his father into his robe—not a bathrobe, but his black judicial robe. The Judge is a very proud man. There is only one robe for him.

The Chaplain and I are enjoying the planning, the fun, the excitement, and the family memories that are being created before our eyes.

I am reminded of Linda Ellis's poem "The Dash," which reminds us that tombstones reveal the date of a person's birth, followed by a dash and the date of death.

What matters most, she reminds us, is how we live, love, and spend our time during the time represented by the dash, the years between birth and death. As the Chaplain and I witness a memory-making and important moment in our friend's ninety-two year-dash, I marvel at how rich his life has been, how beautifully he has lived through his "dash years." He obviously serves as a revered model for all the Hanks—and all the others—in his family. I cannot begin to imagine how many other lives he has touched during this lifetime.

> So, when your eulogy is being read,
> with your life's actions to rehash...
> would you be proud of the things they say
> about how you spent YOUR dash?
> —Linda Ellis

As we rise to leave, Hank Junior introduces his family and thanks us for all the IDT services. This is when we learn something else about the broad and deep impact of The Judge's legacy. Like his father, Hank Junior is a judge. His son, Hank III, is a law professor. Hank IV has just graduated from law school. As he launches his law practice, he is launching a new phase in his life: fatherhood.

Hank Junior grins at the newest Hank in the family. "They come with a whole new set of directions, don't they?" he observes. I smile. "They sure do." I chat about my own new-mother days, when babies were placed on their tummies. "Now, in my new grandmother days, we're told babies should lie on their backs. And that's just the start of the changes we experience in our lives."

" Did your Nurse tell you that we may have swayed him to the profession of law? " asks Hank IV, the new father. I am caught off guard, wondering what he's talking about. He sees my confusion and explains, "I was here visiting The Judge one day and your Nurse and I started talking. It seems he is considering combining two interests: nursing and law. I told him that I was getting ready to hire a nurse as a legal nurse consultant for medical malpractice cases."

I thought about the possibilities a new course of study could open for our valued team member and realized that a nursing-law combination would be a perfect fit for this man. He had come to Hospice after working in a hospital emergency room. He had also cared for his terminally ill father. Those experiences encouraged Nurse to consider broadening his career tracks. I could imagine him successfully investigating accidents and injuries with his unique perspective and background.

When Hospice team members say we benefit as much—or more than—our patients, they know what they're talking about. The greatest benefits of all are life lessons that we can apply to our own lives.

From the cookie jar

"It is your career, so own your own mission statement."

Chapter 7

Annette

On a beautiful early August morning, our Social Worker and I drive down a gravel lane leading to an old two-story home. As we approach, I see our Chaplain in the middle of the road taking a picture of the mailbox. *Well*, I think, *there must be a story here*. We slow the car and stop beside him.

"What are you doing?" I ask.

He explains that our Volunteer is helping Annette—Nettie—with a project. They need a picture of the mailbox, but neither of them has a camera. "So, I offered," he explains.

No doubt in my mind and another yellow hand on the board!

We park the car and stroll up the sidewalk, enjoying the sounds, smells, and sights of an exceptionally beautiful yard. Colorful blooms with intoxicating fragrances overflow in flower beds and terracotta pots. These gardens are as lovely as I have ever seen.

Nettie is sixty-eight, a charming lady who obviously has a green thumb and a passion for using it. Her HHA has just helped her finish her bath. Nettie smells of lilac-scented lotion, and it is immediately apparent to us all that she feels peaceful and she is not in pain from her bone cancer at the moment but it is a nasty disease. We find her sitting at the kitchen table eating pudding. When I compliment her on her beautiful flower garden, she starts to tell her story—not the story about her terminal illness, but about her plans for the "girls," as she calls her daughters.

Nettie tells us that her husband died early in the marriage, leaving her to raise their two very young daughters in this home. Throughout their girlhood, Nettie and her daughters planted flowers, herbs, and vegetables. Annie and Laura are now adults with families of their own, living in other states. Nettie smiles and giggles when she talks about the ways they bonded over pulling weeds. Her personality infuses her stories and her home. She tells us that she spent her career indoors, as a secretary, but as soon as she arrived home at the end of the day, she headed to her yard. "This is where I really thrived," she says.

We help Nettie to the screened back porch, which is where she and our Social Worker always talk so they can enjoy the sights just beyond the porch. I can see why they choose this spot. I, too, love looking at the gardens.

In fact, on a recent visit home, Nettie's daughters had created an old-fashioned outdoor bedroom for their mother on the porch. They moved a cot with a thick soft mattress out there, arranging pillows and summer-weight blankets so their mother could feel cool breezes on her face, smell the blooms just out of reach, and watch her gardens grow. This is what my grandmother used to call a sleeping porch and I am reminded of that special room. I mention this to Nettie, who looks at me seriously for a moment and says, "No hospital rooms and no hospital smells for me ever again. This is where I belong."

I nod. I totally understand. This lovely woman chooses to end her days with the joy involved in having created and nurtured something that will continue to live and grow.

But Nettie isn't ready to stop giving. She carefully explains her plan for the way she plans to spend the rest of her time at home. She is creating identical albums for her daughters.

Thanks to our Volunteer's efforts, the cover of Nettie's album will feature a picture of the old rural mailbox, which reads in big block letters, ANNETTE JACKSON. Nettie explains that when they were little, her girls hand-painted their mother's name there. Now, gorgeous pink roses twist and turn over the mailbox and its post. A small sprig had grown into a beautiful trailing vine over the years. I feel my heart do a little dance as I consider the legacy Nettie is planning for her beloved daughters.

The following pages of the album will feature pictures of Nettie's different flower beds and herb gardens, accompanied by directions for growing them. The album will also include Nettie's special recipes, she tells me. Then, as we sit together quietly on the porch, my eyes travel across the little back yard and the neat rows of lettuce, tomatoes, peppers, and other vegetables. I notice that one area is sectioned off with herbs. Small metal stakes identify each one: rosemary, dill, sweet basil, parsley, chives, oregano. Their fragrances mingle in the summer air just as their various shades of green tempt a cook to harvest them and prepare to chop them into an heirloom recipe.

"The directions in my albums will explain how to plant each plant, their sun requirements (or not), and when to water them," Nettie says, breaking the silence. "I'm going to include every little detail I can think of, to pass as much as I can to my girls." She tells me that Savannah, who is her best friend, and a Hospice Volunteer plan to start digging up "starts" of each plant and herb to give to the girls on their next visit. I can smell the fragrance of a peony bush and more heirloom roses that border the porch. This is Nettie's paradise and Nettie's gift of remembrance to her girls. We'll help her get this legacy documented.

Savannah serves us real lemonade with thin slices of lemon floating among the crushed ice. Nettie and Savannah have been friends since kindergarten, she says. "I'll stay as long as Nettie needs me, since the girls live so far away," she says. Nettie doesn't have to tell me that Savannah is gifted with a warm and compassionate heart—a heart that is very much needed in this home.

Patients and caregivers alike have good days and not-so-good days as they work together through the process of a terminal illness.

Nettie and Savannah smile at each other then Nettie tells us to start writing, she has recipes to share and Savannah will cut us some herbs. We tell her not to go to any trouble but secretly we can't wait to see what she is about to share. It is her way to give back to us and we are honored.

Basic Cream Sauce
2 tablespoons butter
2 tablespoons flour
1 cup milk
1/3 cup heavy cream
dash of salt and pepper
1/4 cup parmesan
Blend together over low heat. Add a handful of fresh herbs of your choice. Mix with any pasta. Enjoy!

Herb Dressing
2 egg yolks beaten
1 cup olive oil
1 Tablespoon wine vinegar
2 Tablespoons chopped parsley
1 Tablespoon each of thyme, lemon balm, tarragon and garlic
Blend and serve over greens.

Omelet Combinations
- Eggs with tomato, parsley and brie
- Eggs with sweet basil and white cheddar
- Eggs with parsley, chives and cheddar

Best Summer Sandwich Ever
Thick slices of a ripe summer tomato
 Generous helping of mozzarella cheese slices
Fresh chopped sweet basil
Grilled on thick slices of buttered sourdough bread.

I know without a doubt that Annie and Laura will cherish the album they will receive one day soon from their very special mother. We are indescribably pleased to play a small role in the process. Nettie's girls will realize that when the time comes, their mother won't be gone from their lives entirely, because she will be everywhere her girls look. Nettie has enriched their lives—and will continue to enrich their lives—with her wisdom and life lessons. With her album, as well as throughout her life, she has given her daughters both roots and wings.

From the cookie jar

"A house is always a home when it offers shelter to your body and gives comfort to your soul."

Chapter 8

Dave

Dave and Fiona are soul mates. Dave and his big red fire truck are soul mates.

When I met Dave, his first words to me were memorable and deeply revealing of his character: "It's not about me, you know."

I smiled in understanding and then he proceeded to tell me his story.

When he heard his diagnosis, a brain tumor, Dave pursued every treatment and every option possible for remission. Without success, he explains. Today, despite being propped up in a hospital bed in the middle of his living room, he is brimming with courage. This space has been converted to meet his needs and to accommodate visits from his firehouse buddies.

The original artwork has been removed from the wall. In its place hang two large posters, one a picture of a big red fire truck with a flag proudly flying, the other a picture of a bright red pickup truck, also with a flag flying in the wind. It seems that when Dave wasn't at the firehouse, he was driving his other beloved red truck.

"Being a fireman was my dream ever since I was a boy," he tells me. "But that's not the only love of my life. I married the right girl."

Despite his illness, one visit to Dave's house convinces me that he and Fiona love life. They have made their home into a gathering place that is usually full of people when they aren't at work. Fiona and another fireman's wife own a small, very successful knitting shop. These days Fiona spends time making plans for the business or knitting for customers in her dining room, so she can be close to Dave. "He is the hero of my heart," she says.

Only fifty-six , Dave is equally dedicated to his two most important roles: as husband and fireman. "It's hard for me to find myself this way," he admits, gesturing to the hospital bed and his pajamas. Until his diagnosis, Dave and his firemen friends worked out frequently and enthusiastically. "Firemen have to stay in excellent condition if we're going to be able to carry the sixty-plus pounds of equipment on our backs needed at a fire," he says. But he doesn't need to tell me how his once-powerful body is becoming progressively weaker and how the disease has compromised him. Dave is a proud man and it took a lot for him to let us help him. The man who was used to running to the aid of others, protecting and serving his community has become a man who needs the help of others.

The team members tell me that every time they visit him, Dave reminds them about fire safety. He talks about the tragedies that take place during fires that could have been prevented. He urges us to change the batteries in our smoke alarms routinely, and he cautions that hot logs in fireplaces can hurtle sparks onto the carpet and start fires. He frequently talks about his love of children and his professional visits to schools. To generations of school children, he has taught the stop-drop-and-roll maneuver that can prevent severe burns. These are not only life lessons, but life-saving lessons. We listen. We learn. And we promise to promote fire safety.

Today, I visit Dave with our Chaplain. He and Dave pray and talk quietly while I wait with Fiona. She is assertive and confident. "I'm fine," she says in answer to my concern, but I notice the dark shadows under her eyes. The IDT will continue to reach out to her.

Suddenly, the peace that envelopes the house evaporates when several big strong guys appear at the door. I smell pizza and see a six pack of beer. One of Dave's friends clicks on the big-screen TV and finds the channel that will broadcast the game they plan to watch together. Dave's band of brothers look tired. Fiona tells me they have just gotten off a long shift. "But they always stop here before going home to their other families," she says.

Dave asks his friends about the shift, and I can hear the longing in his voice. They tell him about the runs they made. It is apparent to me that they work hard to stay connected to Dave and to make certain Dave remains as connected as possible to his past life. His friends ask his advice about something, and a smile flashes across his face before he answers.

It is so important to still feel needed.

As we leave, I notice an open beer can beside Dave on the over bed table. He doesn't drink it or eat any pizza, but the friends know the importance of including him in every way possible. I can tell, beyond a shadow of a doubt, that these men will share the twenty-four-hour watch at the end. And I know they will continue to watch over Dave's wife Fiona.

From the cookie jar

*" This life is yours.
Take the power to choose whatever you
want to do and do it well."*

Susan Polis Schultz

Chapter 9

Miss Sanders

I meet the lovely Miss Sanders, who is in her late eighties, one cool fall afternoon. She is sitting in a rocking chair swathed in quilts. An ancient gold-colored cat named Queenie snoozes in her lap as we conduct a long conversation debating the merits of library cards and e-readers.

Miss Sanders has been a school librarian her entire career. "I love books," she says enthusiastically. "I love the feel of a book, the turn of the pages, the smell of books, and the idea that many people—perhaps even thousands of people—have held the book before me." The e-reader is an entirely new concept to this librarian. "I decided to wait and see how it works out—but I feel sure it will fail," she predicts. "After all, who can resist a real book? "

Miss Sanders fascinates our entire team. She is renowned for her marvelous stories, which she shares while team members give her baths, discuss her needs, adjust her oxygen levels, and check doses of her medications.

Jazz saxophonist and composer John Coltrane is a long-time favorite of Miss Sanders, and his music pours out of a vintage phonograph sitting in her living room. At one point, she speaks quietly of a long lost love. An old black-and-white photograph of a man in uniform sits on a nearby table, a vase of fresh daisies beside it. We aren't sure if her severe heart condition is clinical or emotional, but it is evident that our new friend's heart is broken beyond repair.

Yet this woman who aged the way every woman hopes to age: with grace and pride—characteristics that all who visit her must secretly (or not-so-secretly) envy. Everyone who meets her loves her. She must have been a tremendous influence and inspiration to generations of school children . "Reading," she says, "gives you the opportunity to travel the world, have a new best friend, and never be alone through a story."

Although we see a decline in her health every time we visit Miss Sanders, on her good days she still plays bridge with "the ladies," as she calls her friends. Over a hand of cards, these retired teachers discuss the old days and what became of "our kids," as they call generations of students. After their retirement, many of them missed teaching too much to give it up. They tutored children for years after leaving their classrooms.

Miss Sanders has hired a caregiver, who has moved into her home to assist with daily care and to prevent her from being alone at night. Both she and Nurse have taken such an interest in Miss Sander's stories that they discuss the possibility of volunteering for a literacy program. "You would be surprised at the vast number of people who still don't know how to read," Miss Sanders says, pleased at their idea.

"I'd like to help others learn how to read on behalf of Miss Sanders," Nurse tells me later. I am immensely proud of her and her new goal.

Another yellow hand on the board.

Several weeks after my first visit with Miss Sanders, Nurse asks to talk with me. I assume it is about her new volunteer literacy project, but I am wrong. "Miss Sanders says she'd like to give Queenie to me," Nurse says. A Hospice regulation clearly states that we never accept gifts with more than a ten-dollar value from patients. "Can I accept this gift of Queenie?" she asks.

I tell her that this is a special exception, that we cannot put a dollar value on Queenie. "The most valuable gift is the trust that Miss Sanders has in you," I tell Nurse. "She trusts her precious cat to your care and home. That is a wonderful gift in itself."

Much later, I learn than Nurse takes Queenie to visit Miss Sanders once a week in the evenings on her own time.

From the cookie jar

"Not in her goals, but in her actual transitions, is a woman great, so give credit where credit is due. "

Chapter 10

Mark

As a little girl, I loved going fishing with my Dad. I loved everything about the day and about fishing—except the worms. It was inevitable that I would meet Mark, a young sixty-eight-year-old man who spent every summer fishing and teaching the art of fishing from his boat. He is a retired junior high school teacher, and I knew the moment I met him that Mark is obviously a man who cherishes many fish stories—stories that I feel privileged to hear.

As Mark's terminal illness progressed, his home office lost a desk and gained a hospital bed and the other equipment he requires. The art, however, not the furniture, first captured my attention when I first visit the room. Pictures large and small of Mark, his son John, and twin red-headed grandsons Jason and Jasper cover the walls. I see pictures of fishing trips, vacations, boats, portraits of fish hanging on fishing lines held by toothless grinning little boys, trophies, plaques, and ribbons there. Mark's " fishing time " was well documented. That room represents another world, one in which family time is priceless.

Nurse makes introductions. Mark is sitting in his wheelchair at a card table covered with small pieces of wire, tiny feathers, and beads making fishing lures— and he is having fun with his project.

When I ask him about the art of lure-making, he grins and proceeds to tell me his story. He is a little short of breath and has to resort to his oxygen tank. He is obviously tired. But he tells me he is truly happy in his "fishing cabin," as he has dubbed the room. "I can't say that I'm not sad about this situation, of course I am, but I've made my peace," he tells me. "I'm choosing to let go in my own way."

Mark's wife Brenda serves him hot cocoa in a large ceramic mug with a fish painted on the side. He thanks her and winks at us. "This is the real deal: cocoa, milk, sugar and big puffy marshmallows, not those little packets you add water to," he says. "The boys and I drink it all the time while we work on fishing lures and talk about life." *This man is the real deal, too, not just the cocoa,* I realize. *He has so much to share and he has an audience ready to listen.*

As we talk, I continue to notice his equipment: a pair of waders, fishing poles propped in a corner, tackle boxes, and nets hanging on a hook. But it is the bowl of water with two gold fish swimming around that touches my heart. "The boys," Mark says, gesturing towards the two fish, "gave me these fish to remind me of them—as if I could forget them."

I realize the connection he is making so beautifully: his two little grandsons are two little fish in the big pond of life.

Lots of lessons were being taught in this fishing cabin because people are talking to each other.

Nurse discusses Mark's needs, then schedules the next visit. Mark turns to me and says, "Hospice gives me time. No hospital would let me enjoy all of this." His eyes sweep the room. "Hospitals won't let the little boys visit because they are too young. The nurses would wake me up at all hours to take my temperature, pulse and weigh me. Who cares at this point how much I weigh? I just need my family, some good fish stories, and a little more time around here. Hospice offers me that chance, and keeps me comfortable. Please put that in your advertisements."

"Yes, sir," I promise " and, you just put into words why we do this everyday."

From the cookie jar

"He looked the truth straight on."

Coach Vince Lombardi of the Green Bay Packers

Chapter 11

Sally

The old white farmhouse faces a dusty gravel road. On this hot August afternoon, by the entrance to the farm lane sits a long table with a handwritten sign announcing FARMER'S MARKET. Baskets of corn, green beans, melons, red and green peppers, and tomatoes are displayed under a large green-and-white striped market umbrella. In the middle of the table shoppers will find a large mason jar with a sign taped to it saying, "Honor System." Nurse and I stop to admire the produce and notice that the jar is filled with dollar bills and coins.

Well, I think, *another valuable life lesson*.

The farmhouse is typical of countless farmhouses in the Midwest. Two stories tall, it features a big porch that stretches across the front of the home. Rocking chairs line the porch. Bright yellow flowers and vines overflow the window boxes. Wildflowers follow the driveway to the house, gently swaying in the hot summer breeze. Our car joins an old blue pickup truck and a new white BMW beside the house.

I know that Sally, who is thirty-two, has been fighting leukemia for two frustrating years. The diagnosis interrupted a fast-track career in advertising. After earning her MBA, she followed her dream and moved to the big city, where she landed a job she loved. Now she has come home to the farm during her leave of absence.

The Sally that I meet has a cute pixie hair style. Her newly grown-out hair is blond. She is pale, thin, and bruised, but she is also funny and full of spirit. "I've traded my suits and stiletto heels for my orange capri pajamas and flip-flops. My best friend packed me up and drove me home in my brand new car." My friends' parting words were, 'Stay off your laptop and cell phone. Rest and let your Mom take care of you, " she tells me when we're introduced.

Then Sally adds, "You can imagine my surprise. I spend years going to school so I can get away from the farm, doing yoga and dieting to stay in shape, only to find myself back on the farm and skinny—no dieting required. " The irony of it all.

Clearly, she is adored by her parents. We sit together in their comfortable living room. Here, everywhere you look, your eyes skim over photographs documenting Sally's many achievements. The room is lovely and the atmosphere is loving. Even the crazy cuckoo in the clock seems to enjoy being here; he appears every fifteen minutes.

I venture into the kitchen while Nurse examines Sally. Here, boots line up at the back door and a peg rack is loaded with jackets. Sally's mother and I sit at a long oak farm table lined with high-back chairs. This is obviously the heart of the family home and the location of all discussions. As if reading my mind, she talks about Sally's school projects that took shape at this table. Atop the big five-burner stove sits a huge pot. I can smell homemade soup simmering. Meanwhile, the oven exudes the aromas of real buttermilk biscuits baking. "I'm making all Sally's favorite foods, in hopes that she'll start eating again," she says.

After a moment, in a change of voice, she confesses, "We encouraged her in school. We wanted her to achieve all of her goals. We always knew we would lose her to the big city, but we didn't know we would lose her," her voice cracks and she pauses for a moment before she raises her chin and adds, "But we still hope another drug or another new treatment will cure her."

I put my arms around Sally's mother. "I've learned over the years that people do recover, so you never take away hope," I say.

A few minutes later, Nurse and I trade places. She speaks with Sally's Mom about any additional support they may need. I help Sally to the rocking chairs on the porch, and we choose our seats, rocking while we admire the farm. Green fields stretch as far as we can see. We glimpse her father in the distance, working near a barn.

"Tell me about the honor system," I ask.

"Well, we sell the extra produce that we don't send out to the groceries," Sally explains. "Neighbors come by every day to buy what they need for their families. My parents believe that if someone takes something without paying for it or takes the money from the jar then they must really need it. So, end of discussion."

Then, Sally sits silently for long minutes, gazing around the farm she knows so well. She sighs. "Well, if this is God's way to slow me down, I've heard him loud and clear," she says. "I'm good with the plan. But, oh how I hope I can have a bone marrow transplant or anything else so I can get well."

The fact that Sally has been referred to Hospice pretty much tells her story—at this moment. But things can change quickly. Miracles do happen.

I ask about her career, and her face lights up. She talks about the advertising industry, climbing the corporate ladder, and working sixty-plus hour weeks. Then she says, "I've traded my laptop, e-mail, and constant texting for playing cards and watching old black-and-white movies with Mom and Dad, who insist that these are the only movies that have real actors." She laughs quietly, adding, "Now that I'm home, I have no deadlines and no meetings. I've never slept better than I do here. This land is quiet. I once thought I loved the sounds of city traffic, but not so much anymore."

She tells me that the next day her sorority sisters are arriving, to visit for a few days. "Simple pleasures," she observes. "Mom's cooking and real face-to-face conversation. No carry-out boxes of Chinese, texting, and e-mails. Just the pleasures of home cooking and a home wrapped in TLC. "

Sally's Childhood Favorite Breakfast: Toad in a Hole
Cut a hole out of the center of a slice of break. Melt butter on a grill. Lay the bread on the grill. Break an egg into the hole in the center. Sprinkle it with salt & pepper. Toast about 2 minutes. Flip and cook another minute.

A few weeks after first visit to the farm, our team members are thrilled to discharge Sally from our Hospice services so she can once again pursue aggressive treatment. This time her body responds well. We learn Sally has been told she is in remission. We are elated, and we celebrate the news during our weekly meeting.

During the next few months, Sally calls frequently. In one conversation, she reveals that as she continues to recover, she is re-thinking her career. "I love the advertising business, but I plan to slow my life down,' she says. "Life is just too precious to rush through it."

From the cookie jar

"Sharing and caring are spontaneous gifts available to us every day. At this farm, it is called The Honor System."

Chapter 12

Matt

At the age of forty-four, Matt's plan for his life suddenly required a dramatic revision—as well as the support and camaraderie of family and friends, if he wanted to accomplish his goal. When he was diagnosed with a terminal illness, he took the words of President Franklin D. Roosevelt to heart: "We may not be able to prepare the future for our children, but we can at least prepare our children for the future. "

Matt and his wife Jen are both accomplished architects who love projects. Their home is a vintage two-story brick that provides a continuous "to do" list of projects. It has tall narrow windows, rough plaster walls, and wood floors with a beautiful aged patina. Outdoors, the sidewalk snakes to the front door, composed of uneven bricks flanked by ivy.

"Old houses make me smile because they are so soulful," Matt says. But, truly, for Matt and Jen their true love is Sam, their only child. At fourteen, Sam is a mini-Matt. He is tall for his age, with dark curly hair and snappy eyes that light up when he is excited about something.

The first time we meet, Matt is less interested in talking about his colon cancer with Nurse and more interested—and agitated—about his garage. I have no idea what is going on in the garage, but I soon learn that it will earn some of my team members a yellow hand on the wall in the conference room.

It seems that one day while Nurse visited the home, she learned about a project that had consumed the time and attention of both Matt and Sam every weekend prior to Matt's diagnosis. Matt had discovered a vintage Mustang in a heap of parts and rust. Together the father and son were restoring the car, step by step. Matt's goal was quality time together. The deadline? Sam's sixteenth birthday. Now Matt's only concern appeared to be the pile of parts sitting in the garage, a project that he could no longer work on with Sam.

Hearing their story, Nurse talked to our Volunteer Coordinator, who set the wheels in motion—literally. She knew that one of our Volunteers had experience working with cars, and she made a few calls. Volunteers were quick to come to the Mustang's rescue. They arranged a meeting with Matt and struck up a deal. Matt would tell them how he wanted the project done, and they would provide the labor to carry out Matt's plan.

Meanwhile, Matt talked with his buddies, who assured them they would take Sam under their wing, promising to talk to him about important boy topics, girls, college, fraternities, money, you name it. But Matt was equally concerned about Jen, who is crushed by her grief. "She acts like everything is normal, but of course it isn't," Matt tells us. I know that she had refused to talk with our Social Worker and Chaplain. "She has lots of friends and colleagues, but will she let them help her? That is my biggest question," Matt confesses.

I learn that one evening Sam came to Matt and said as only kids can, "Dad, please don't be mad at me, but I did something Mom won't like. Please don't be mad."

Sam then confessed that he had launched an internet search for his mother's sister. She and Kim hadn't spoken in ten years. "Probably neither one even remembered why they fought in the first place," Matt tells us. "Sam barely remembered her visits, but in his quest to help his Mom, he felt compelled to find Kim."

Matt, much too weak this late in the evening to sit up, thought to himself, "Wow, the wisdom of kids!" What he did say was, "Sam, come here and give me a hug." Then he asked, "Did you find Kim?"

Sam grinned." I sure did. She'll be here in an hour."

Much later that evening, after the drama subsided, Jen and Kim couldn't thank Sam enough. "I now feel that Jen has the support she still doesn't acknowledge she'll need," Matt tells the team.

From the cookie jar

"Family and friends are more valuable than gold. "

Chapter 13

Janet

O n this humid early morning in the summer, I am riding to the hospital with Nurse to see a new patient referral. All we know is that Janet is fifty-six, she has end-stage liver cancer, and she has elected to accept Hospice service.

What we encounter as we enter the hospital room is a very agitated lady and a man trying to soothe her without much success.

Before we can even introduce ourselves, the woman says, "Get me out of here. Please just get me out of here!" We hurry to explain the program, inform her of her insurance approval, and explain how we can provide care while she is in her own home.

She seems to relax before our eyes. She then introduces us to Kyle, her ex-husband. Whatever had happened between them in the past seemed over and done now. It is apparent to us that they are close friends. We obtain a discharge order and instruct Kyle to take Janet home. "We'll meet you there to do the admission," we say. We watch as Janet tucks her arm under Kyle's elbow. She leans against him for support as they wait for a wheelchair and an Aide to wheel her out of the hospital room to his car.

When we arrive, I can see why Janet wanted to be home. She is an artist and surrounds herself with color. The stark white hospital walls, white sheets, and cold tile floors must have been very depressing for her, even though she had been re-admitted for only two days, in an effort to control her symptoms. Clearly, it had been two days too many.

Janet notices us admiring her home and says, "Never again will I go to a hospital. I just want to be home with my things." Kyle smiles at her and says, "Well, I guess I'm a 'thing' now, and that's okay with me."

Kyle nestles Janet in the pink sheets of her big four poster canopy bed. A colorful vintage quilt lies folded at the foot of the bed.

I walk with Kyle to the kitchen while Nurse starts her examination and admission paperwork. My eyes darted around the room. These walls are painted a bright egg-yolk yellow. A recipe for sugar cookies is stenciled around the upper wall as a border. Often an individual's decorating style says more than the individual about priorities, values, and life style. This kitchen is adorable. A vision of Janet begins to take shape in my mind.

Janet's Sugar Cookies
1 cup shortening
2/3 cup sugar
1/4 teaspoon salt
2 teaspoons vanilla
2 eggs
2 1/2 cups flour

Mix all ingredients together, then roll dough on floured board. Cut into shapes. Bake at 375 degrees for 8 minutes. Cool. Spread with icing and sprinkles.

"Calories are not counted for cookies in this home. "

On the counter a bright red Kitchen Aid mixer waits to be turned on. Sun streams through the kitchen windows. I see a hammock strung between two towering trees in the back yard. Kyle tells me that Janet spends a lot of time out there. "The hammock seems to mold to her back in a way that gives her comfort. But mostly, I think, she loves the colors of the yard and the blue sky," he says quietly.

Nurse finishes the admission and we chat with Kyle about how to contact us for any needs. We promise to stop by at the end of the day just to be sure Janet is settled.

Before we leave, I tiptoe into the bedroom to say goodbye to Janet. The lights are off and the window shades are drawn. I catch my breath. Janet is wearing bright purple pj's. Tiny white lights are strung around the bedposts and through the canopy. The sight is like a wonderland, soft and pretty. Janet is sound asleep. As we quietly exit the room, Kyle whispers, "Janet doesn't want the room totally dark. She says these tiny flecks of light remind her of her childhood and lightening bugs."

I smile. Hospice has given Janet peace and comfort in her home. We are doing our job.

We speak with Kyle at length before we leave. We know that caregivers need to share and vent their thoughts, concerns, and impressions. Kyle tells us he is a policeman, a job that forced Janet to worry constantly about his safety. She asked him to take a desk job, but he told her he loved working on the streets. "The issue brought so much tension and stress to our lives that we divorced. But we continued to love each other. This situation has brought us back to each other," he says. He speaks about the guilt he is feeling. Janet had worried about the dangers inherent in her husband's job, that he could get shot and die. Instead, she became sick and he will be the one to lose his love.

"She didn't do anything to deserve this," he says. We can hear the frustration and despair in his voice.

"We know," Nurse and I say at the same time.

Much later in our day, we return to Janet's home to make sure she is all set for the weekend and to review the process of calling the answering service if she needs anything.

Janet's sister Lisa and her young daughters Mellie and Molly meet us at the door. Lisa has baked sugar cookies, and the four family members are seated at the kitchen table dunking cookies in glasses of cold milk while playing Old Maid with a well worn deck of cards. The girls are giggling and I laugh and tell them, "I love the fact that in this world of computer games, families still play cards and board games." The girls offer us friendship bracelets woven from bright colored thread.

The little things mean so much.

I notice an easel standing in the corner of the kitchen and a canvas work-in-progress. The word FORGIVE is painted in bright crayola colors across the top. The outline of two people overlapping is taking shape. I suspect that the two people are Janet and Kyle, and Janet is painting a gift for him. I'm in awe of her spirit. Forgiveness is a powerful emotion. Janet is happy to be home where she is surrounded by people who love her.

From the cookie jar

"Even in the most desperate situations, we see perspective and recognize the need to have peace within ourselves."

Chapter 14

Bobby

I am a little surprised when our Home Health Aide and I pull up in front of a little Mom-and-Pop-type ice cream store. She is wearing a huge smile on her face when she announces that this is where Bobby lives.

I look at her skeptically, and she laughs again. "Well," she admits, "he actually lives upstairs over the store."

A big bright sign swinging in the breeze says " SCOOPS. " Small tables and chairs inside the shop are filled with families who are obviously enjoying themselves. The children look happy and very contented, most little faces smeared with ice cream.

"Let's go in and say hello first. Then we'll go upstairs to visit with Bobby, " suggests the HHA.

We greet Rosa, Bobby's wife, who is the party planner for the children's parties SCOOPS hosts. Working with her is Tad, Bobby's brother. He explains that he usually handles the business side of the SCOOPS, but now he is doing double duty as a scooper, taking Bobby's place.

SCOOPS' walls are covered in colorful drawings and riddles, but I can tell that our HHA has more secrets up her sleeve, secrets she is not yet prepared to reveal.

We climb the old stairs and I meet Bobby, who has lung cancer and is sitting in a lounge chair. He is pale, sweating, and uncomfortable. We spring into action, calling Nurse, who arrives quickly. She consults with our Medical Director and makes adjustments to Bobby's medications as well as his oxygen level. I sit and hold his hand until I see relief start to spread over his face. When he seems comfortable, I stand and prepare to tiptoe out of the room so he can rest, but he pulls me back and says, "Don't leave me. I haven't told you about SCOOPS yet."

HHA and I return to our seats and quickly discover we are going to be treated to one of the greatest stories. Bobby tells us that he and Tad are third-generation owners of SCOOPS and that there is a story about the wall décor. "When I was young, I wanted to be a teacher," Bobby says, "but family tradition dictated that I work at SCOOPS with Tad. So, I decided to create a way to do both."

Every day, he explains, he asks visiting children a question. If they answer correctly, they are rewarded with a free dip of ice cream. They write the question and answer on the wall in a bright colorful marker and sign their name.

"What kind of questions?" I ask.

"Real easy questions for the little ones," he says. "Like spelling their names, or maybe what 2 +2 equals. Then, for grade schoolers, I might ask the capital of a state, who made the flag, or a math problem."

I am impressed. Bobby is so proud.

When Bobby has a good day now, he has a special chair in the ice cream shop where he sits and talks to visitors, he tells me. Like a warm-weather Santa, he draws children to him.

HHA and I prepare to leave, each with a dip of fresh strawberry ice cream in a sugar cone. When we reach the car, I sit and reflect on this wonderful story. Bobby is ill, but he continues to offer so much to the children who visit his store.

Bobby offers a powerful lesson in positive attitude and determination.

From the cookie jar

"It is never too late in the day to become the person you really wanted to be."

Chapter 15

Mazie

This winter day is particularly cold. Snow is falling faster than the windshield wipers can clear it. Nurse and I are on our way to meet a new referral from an inner-city clinic.

We arrive at the address of an aged boarding house that has clearly seen better days. The entire structure appears to be in danger of falling apart. We climb two flights of stairs and knock on the door of the apartment.

After a few minutes, we hear the familiar sound of a walker scraping across the floor. A faint voice calls, "One moment, please." And then the door opens. We carry in the sack of oranges that is lying beside the door.

Mazie is as tiny as her one-room apartment, but her spirit is extraordinary—bigger than anything I've seen recently. A long gray braid stretches down her back. She is dressed in layers to stay warm. Her apartment is spotless, but it has minimal furniture. We notice that her couch is a nest of pillows and blankets. She sleeps there.

At Mazie's suggestion, we sit at a card table to discuss the Hospice program. She speaks about the clinic where she had received care for her renal disease, the length and progress of her illness, medication that doesn't help anymore, and how she "just might need a little help now."

We explain Hospice and the team who will be caring for her. In her earlier life, she had worked outside the home, she says, so she receives a small Social Security check and Medicare coverage. Electing the Hospice benefit will give her medications, necessary equipment, and a team of caring professionals to oversee her care. "This is more than I could even imagine," she marvels.

Nurse begins her examination and admission paperwork. I excuse myself and stroll around the building for a few minutes, to give them privacy. When I return, a bag containing two pairs of warm socks is hanging on the doorknob.

We ask Mazie about family and friends who might be able to stay with her if she needs their help. She smiles and says, "If needed, that won't be a problem." We notice that there is no phone in the apartment, and we ask how she can call us in an emergency. Again she smiles and says, "If needed, that won't be a problem." It seems that food appears magically and daily from friends.

Nurse schedules Mazie's next appointment and makes notes to speak with our Medical Director about medications. We learn that a friend had dropped off the walker so Mazie would be safer in her apartment. Nurse adjusts its height and instructs Mazie about its use. "I'll order you a hospital bed," she says. "It will be so much more comfortable than sleeping on the couch."

I think of the challenge the movers will face when they try carrying a hospital bed up the narrow and rickety flight of stairs. *Well, that has been done before and will be done again,* I remind myself. I notice a tear sliding down Mazie's cheek, and I hazard a guess that it has been a long time since Mazie slept in a bed of any kind.

Several days later, our Social Worker shares an interesting story during our team meeting. She has met Mazie and tells us that Mazie has lived in her tiny apartment for nearly twenty years. "She has a host of friends in the building and from the streets who keep watch over her," she says. "Food arrives and her medications are picked up for her." We learn that Mazie hasn't been able to leave her apartment for three months.

We also learn that before she became so ill, this almost-eighty-year-old woman walked several blocks two times a week to serve food at a homeless shelter. She explained to our Social Worker, "Everyone should give where they can." Because she had been so grateful for her home, despite its small size and decrepit appearance, she felt compelled to give to those who have no home at all.

We shake our heads and add this to life lessons learned.

From the cookie jar

*"Leading by example comes to us
in many ways."*

Chapter 16

The Reverend Jack Mitchell

The Reverend Jack Mitchell is in his late fifties. Tall and blessed with an athletic build, it is apparent that he was once far more active than he finds himself now, on the other side of healthy.

We drive to a neat white parish house with black shutters and a front door that opens all day long to welcome guests. Nurse and I enter the lovely home and are shown to a side parlor that has become a bedroom for Rev Mitchell.

He looks comfortable sitting in a reclining chair. "I hate to take up your time," he apologizes before we can even greet him.

" What do you mean?" I ask.

"Well, I've counseled so many ill patients and their families that I know what is coming. I'll be all right. I know where I'm going, after all. And you must be very busy," he says, smiling at us.

"I'm not too busy for you," I say, returning his smile and sitting down. "Besides, this is different. I'm here to see you, not someone else."

With those words, his eyes fill with tears. Often Hospice provides the emotional release patients need, we know. For once the Rev doesn't have to be strong for others. We understand terminal illness and his circumstances.

Nurse proceeds with her examination and adjusts some medications while I wait in the living room. It becomes apparent that the reverend has needs, but he is reluctant to accept the help. He is accustomed to being the strong, supportive man in control, not the recipient of assistance. He wants to be angry, but thinks anger is unacceptable because of his faith. Nurses and Doctors can sympathize; often we believe we should be able to take care of ourselves in times of our own medical emergencies, that we shouldn't need assistance from others.

In reality, every one of us needs help at different times in our lives.

When the examination is finished, we talk. I ask Rev Mitchell to tell me his story, explaining, "No two stories are alike. Everyone has a story that needs to be told."

Jack and Trina had been college sweethearts when he received his calling, he tells us. "The rest," he says, "is history." After marriage and Jack's graduation from seminary, they were planted in a wonderful church family and have never moved. They raised their two sons here as they all became part of a supportive extended family. He speaks about memorable baptisms, counseling his congregation, hospital rounds, weddings, house blessings, and funerals.

The reverend is no different from any of us as he tries to plan his remaining time. What bothers him, he says, is that Trina will have to move, since the parish house belongs to the church. The church assures him there will be no rush, but he feels compelled to resolve this issue before he can relax. Our Social Worker has spent hours listening to him sort out details, as she has for so many others.

Over the next few weeks, the Mitchells decide to move into a small condo. "It will be perfect for Trina later," the Rev tells me. He is adamant that they move together, immediately. His church members pack and move them. It is apparent how appreciative and dedicated they are to Rev Mitchell and Trina. "My goal is to be able to bless our new home myself, and to be sure that Trina is safe and settled," he tells me. This becomes the reverend's process of letting go.

Nurse makes several visits a week. Our Chaplain and Rev Mitchell talk often and at great length. "I know where I'm going," he says in a firm voice. And then he adds, "But I'm still trying to put it all in perspective and make peace." He speaks about the lessons life and his faith have taught him—"They are free, if you look and listen," he reminds us.

From the cookie jar

"Your work must feed your soul."

Chapter 17

Chloe

This is one of those gorgeous spring days, warm but not hot. Spring rains have turned the grass emerald green, and all the trees are displaying their new and brightly colored leaves and blossoms. Wild flowers are blooming along the highway and back roads. All the world seems fresh, clean, and lovely.

When Nurse and I arrive at Chloe's home, we immediately realize we are in the presence of a unique lady. The rambling one-story gray cement-block building is both her home and business. To the right of the door hangs a big mailbox with the word RED spelled out in appropriate red block letters.

We ring a bell and two young ladies named Betsy and Denise invite us in. When we are ushered into the hall, we realize that the building has a distinctive floor plan. To the left of the hall we see an office and workroom. To the right is a huge space that has been divided into a living room, kitchen/dining room, bedroom, and bath. It is a clever use of space, and the appearance is very welcoming. We find Chloe sitting in her living room on an old slip-covered couch, wearing matching red pj's and robe. We can tell immediately that she is very much in need of our Nurse, who immediately begins assessing the situation.

Betsy, Denise, and I cross over to the office to chat. The girls are taking turns staying with their aunt, they tell me. I assure them that Nurse will evaluate Chloe and create a new plan of action with our Medical Director. "Chloe is usually full of spirit, even if her energy is running low—as it always seems to be these days," Betsy explains. "It's frightening to see her declining."

I discuss how our team is created, to help not only the patient, but also the family. I assure them that we are on call twenty-four hours a day, seven days a week, and as I speak, I can see them visibly relax.

I ask about Chloe's business. They both grin and promise, "She will tell you all about it when she feels better." "But," Betsy adds, " be prepared to be amazed."

Eventually, we return to the living room and join Nurse and Chloe. Chloe is looking much better. I tell her about the team approach and that I have given the girls the details as well. Nurse explains that Chloe will have the on-call team check on her again this evening, but if she needs anything at all before that, to call the office.

We stand up to leave, but Betsy and Denise both say, "I thought you wanted to know about the business."

"Oh, I do! But, would another day be better? " I ask.

Chloe waves her hand toward our seats and invites us to stay. "Let me tell you why I need Hospice," she suggests. "I have been well until recently, but things are changing quickly."

Of course, we sit down in a hurry.

As Chloe waves a red-painted fingernail towards the office, she tells us, "I've been designing things since I was doodling on lined paper in grade school." Because she had a heart condition as a child, she explains, she was unable to jump rope, hang from the jungle gym at the park, or take dance lessons. As a young adult, she received a heart transplant. By that time, her love for "funky fashion" and drawing had become her passion, and her passion became her career. "I chose the name RED for my business because it's the color of a heart, of course, and the heart has very special meaning to a heart recipient."

Chloe designs purses, tote bags, hats, shawls, and other clothing items, using at least three different fabrics for each project, some of them new, some vintage. "I always incorporate an old piece of jewelry on everything I make, for fun," Chloe says, explaining that she works on the pieces year-round and sells them at art fairs and in local boutiques. "I'm known for the special words printed on the price tag," she adds.

"What kind of words?" Nurse and I ask at the same time.

"In red ink, I write empowerment words," she says. "It might be gratitude, appreciation, respect, politeness, patience, resilience, love. These are words that reflect my priorities, and the price tag becomes a conversation piece with customers."

She turns reflective and speaks more slowly. "I was given an incredible gift when I received another person's heart. But it is almost over now." She smiles at her nieces and tells us, "But my business will go on because both girls love it. They plan to run the business together."

Nurse and I ask about the possibility of another transplant, but Chloe shakes her head. " I had one. Now it's someone else's turn."

Yes, we are amazed.

From the cookie jar

"Life isn't about how to survive the storm, but how to dance in the rain."

Chapter 18

Russell

Late one Friday afternoon, Nurse knocks on my office door and asks if I could take a ride with her the next day. "I know it's Saturday," she adds quickly, "but Russell wants to meet you. He won't tell me why, but he insists it has to be Saturday."

I'm not only curious, I can never deny a patient a visit. "Sure," I say. "What time?"

"It has to be three in the afternoon," she says.

Now my curiosity is really piqued.

That Saturday afternoon, sleet is lashing at the windshield as we drive to the proverbial middle of nowhere, where Russell lives. (Our Hospice accepts patients within fifty miles of our office, from any direction.) We drive down one rural road after another until I am convinced we are lost. Finally, we turn onto a long lane and see an amazingly beautiful log cabin.

"Russell built this himself many years ago," Nurse tells me. Off to the side stands a large barn that houses a semi-truck. To our surprise, the long gravel driveway is lined with cars, SUV's, pickup trucks, and several big rigs with out-of-state license plates. Nurse and I exchange glances, wondering what is happening in that cabin.

The front door opens before we can knock. Russell's wife Sharon welcomes us into their home. She is a pretty petite woman with red hair cut in a bob and eyes that mirror both her sadness and the day's excitement. We stomp our feet before entering, trying to guess what we have walked into.

In the center of the big room sits a hospital bed, where Russell is sitting up and wearing a party hat. Streamers and balloons are everywhere. People swarm through the room with plates of food and cups of beer. The room exudes the supportive spirit of family and friends. The enormous stone fireplace is stacked with blazing logs that crackle and snap and send a warmth into the room and its occupants. A long banner tacked to the mantle announces, "HAPPY 57th BIRTHDAY!"

I cross the room to meet Russell, who is a very big guy with tattoos. He extends a big hand to me and squeezes my hand, telling me how happy he is that we could join his party. A tiny black dog peeks from the blanket covering Russell's lap, and he leans over to kiss her nose. "Her name is Barbie," he tells me, as I try to conceal the look of surprise on my face. This was not the kind of man I would imagine having a small yappy dog named Barbie.

Russell tells me that he has spent his entire career on the road driving big rigs, and Barbie is his fellow traveler. "I couldn't have a big dog in the rig, but Barbie was just the right size. She and I are buddies," he says. The two would arrive home every Friday, then return to the road on Mondays. Until recently, that is, when severe stomach pains and a cancer diagnosis changed his life.

"I've had lots of tests, all kinds of treatments, but the doctors can't find a magic potion for me," he tells us.

I offer our team's help in any and every way possible. Then I stand beside Russell as the crowd of friends sing "Happy Birthday" and watch Sharon cut a huge cake, which is served with homemade ice cream.

Russell smiles broadly as he addresses his family members and friends. "Since my twenties, I've been on the road, so rarely have I been home on my actual birthday," he says. He smiles at his wife. "Sharon planned all of this at my insistence. I know this is my last birthday. I don't want any of you at a funeral. I want a big celebration of life. So party away! "

This is a man whose cup is always half full, never half empty.

At the end of the afternoon, I search for Sharon, to thank her for inviting us. "I want to show you something," she says. We walked to the rear of the cabin and enter a library full of books, tapes and pictures from places Russell had traveled. She smiles and observes, "He surprises you, doesn't he ?"

"Yes, he does." I tell her how much I admire his attitude. "He has superstar quality," I say. "We always hope that Hospice gives people not only the comfort and compassion they deserve, but also the time they need to get their affairs in order. Russell accomplished this his way. I am so pleased to share his birthday with him—and with you."

I ask about the book collection, and Sharon explains that Russell listens to books on tape while he drives. "He can answer just about any question you can think of, and he speaks fluent Spanish, which he learned from language tapes." When I look stunned, she adds, "Since he's been home for a few months, he has started tutoring young kids about the importance of staying in school. He Skypes with a local high school Spanish class, and he tutors some of the students from his bed."

From the cookie jar

"A lot happens in a home besides a terminal illness."

Chapter 19

All The Other Patients

Over the years I have seen hundreds and hundreds of Hospice patients. Like the patients that I have chosen to share in detail, each one has a story that is unique to them.

Hospice patients range in age from sixteen to more than one hundred. They represent all nationalities and customs. They observe a variety of religious and spiritual views. They may have large families. They may have no families. Some have finances to plan an extravagant last trip—but most do not. They are tall. They are short. They are overweight. They are underweight. Some have no hair. Others have a thick crop of blond, brown, black, red, gray or white hair in every imaginable style.

The homes Hospice team members visit are mansions, high-rise condos, ancient sprawling farmhouses, small tract houses, trailers, lodges, cabins, apartments, retirement cottages, or rooms in nursing facilities. The caregivers are as varied as the patients themselves. They can be young or old, friends or family members—while some are frightened, others are at peace. Together they are confronting terminal diseases, which can range from oncology-related illnesses to end-stage diseases—cardiac, renal, respiratory, neurological, or Alzheimer's. Some suffer from the curse of an inherited medical condition. They may have been fighting a disease for years and undergoing aggressive treatment like surgery, radiation, or chemotherapy—repeatedly or for a short time.

The Hospice team becomes part of the family dynamics. Hospice patients are married, divorced, single, share blended families, belong to tight-knit families, or are estranged from siblings and parents. Some patients bring alcohol, drugs, gambling, and smoking addictions with them to Hospice. Some face family struggles, job loss, serious financial concerns, strong differences of opinion, addictions, and fears of the unknown. Too often families want one course of action, while the patient wants another. They may argue, fuss and fight before agreeing or not.

Some patients need personal space. Others need to be surrounded by people. They enjoy every hobby imaginable. Hospice workers quickly become accustomed to the power of pets—and we have seen just about every type of pet you can imagine serving as companions to patients suffering from terminal illnesses.

Some patients stabilize while on Hospice service and choose to undertake another round of aggressive treatment with the newest miracle drug or protocol, so we discharge them. They can be re-admitted at any time—but we hope and pray that the new drug or protocol will make the difference between life and death.

Some ask, "Why me?" Some do not.

Some regret taking the health risks that land them in this situation, such as smoking.

Many fear leaving their family—and that fear is often more traumatic than the disease itself.

Some patients have unresolved issues and need forgiveness in order to face the end with a sense of peace with themselves and others. The ability to forgive is an priceless gift, we have learned.

Letting go is a process. A normal and necessary process.

But, I have yet to meet anyone who isn't happy to be in his or her own home with the support that Hospice offers. We may care for the patient only a few hours or over the course of months. Later, we maintain touch with the family for a year. Our commitment is not just to the patient, but to the patient's entire family, to help them transition to their new future. Many family members and friends return to us as Volunteers.

Our patients represent all walks of life. They are teachers, car salesmen, secretaries, architects, doctors, writers, house painters, nurses, lawyers, cooks, sales reps, singers, actors, artists, athletes, business owners, bankers, taxi drivers, social workers, flight attendants, pilots, landscapers, clergy, realtors, computer programmers, and medical researchers, just to name a few. Whatever their background, however, they share important life lessons with us as we care for them.

From the cookie jar

*" We love them all just as they are.
We move on, but we never ever forget
them or the lessons they teach us."*

Chapter 20

The Team

It was getting late in the day. I had finished my last conference call and e-mailed the daily report. Team members had completed all scheduled patient visits. The on-call team was in the conference room, receiving reports to carry them through the night. I packed my briefcase to go home, but first I completed one final walk through the office, checking that phones had been forwarded, lights had been clicked off, and the coffee pot unplugged. Finally, I walked past the "bull pen," as we call it, where all team member have a cubicle to call their own.

I love the bull pen, with its pictures of our team members' kids, small potted plants, jars of candy on the shelves, charts needing to be completed or "to do" notes pinned to the wall. Many times I see my team members' personal "bucket lists" taped to a shelf or thumb-tacked to a memo board, with something special circled in red. Many of the notations on those lists are inspired by the patients they have seen and the stories they have heard.

Over the years I've had the privilege to work with an ongoing roster of team members, all of whom are beyond dedicated to Hospice and the patients we care for. People don't enter this profession unless they truly and totally care. I chose not to use first names in this book for team members whose experiences I relate because there are so many names and so many personal stories. In this book, as in our professional lives, our focus is on the patient and the family supported by the services of the entire Interdisciplinary Team. And, all patient names have been changed for privacy.

But, you should know that..........

Above all else we respect each other. Here, in this workplace, kindness rules.

We aren't afraid to hold a hand or give a hug to a team member who weeps or shows emotion. We invest caring and compassion in each other as well as our patients and families. Emotional and physical burnout is a serious issue in a profession like ours, so we do everything in our power to share the weight of burdens and emotions.

We see patients in the stifling heat and in blizzard conditions, at any hour of the day or any day of the week, including holidays. We care for people physically, emotionally, and spiritually—and that includes each team member.

The Nurses who choose to work with Hospice are exceptionally skilled and loving caregivers. They work closely with the Medical Director to control symptoms and, at all times, to keep patients comfortable. I once had a Nurse walk through water up to her knees because the road she needed to travel had flooded and she was determined to see a patient in trouble. Several of our Nurses knit preemie hats for a local hospital; they believe this completes the life cycle from their perspective.

Social Workers are the salt of the earth. They have the knowledge, patience, and strength to help patients and families manage the dramatic changes happening in their lives. People in great distress respond in a wide variety of ways. Different personalities present different and changing challenges. Social Workers work hard to smooth and harmonize family dynamics. Sometimes patients want or need to blame someone for their terminal illness. Social Workers understand that this is part of the grieving process. Everyone has a unique story. Social Workers help them carry their personal baggage.

Chaplains have the power to lay a hand on a shoulder and quiet a mind. These dedicated and compassionate individuals pray and listen, allowing patients and families to unload their concerns and find peace.

The Home Health Aides are priceless. I am constantly amazed at the amount of information they can gather during a bath, and the tremendous comfort a bath and a clean pair of pajamas can make in a patient's life. HHAs observe, listen, and respond to patients, then report their findings to our Nurses. They are a vital link in the chain of care.

Every team needs an excellent Bereavement Coordinator, the miracle worker who assists grieving families once the patient's life is over. Bereavement Coordinators are available immediately following a death, and they follow families for a year. Hospice offers individual counseling as well as monthly bereavement groups. I remember eating butterscotch pie every month for a year at the bereavement support meeting because a grieving widow felt compelled to honor her deceased husband and his fondness for butterscotch pie. She needed to make it, so we ate it.

An Admissions Coordinator serves as the link between all the team members. She answers the phone, which often rings constantly. She takes referrals and organizes appointments so the team can meet the patients and their families. Her day is so busy that often she eats lunch at her desk and she rarely takes a break, unless we force her. Her busy schedule is a sign that our outside sales team is doing a great job. And she is tireless as the inside marketer.

Our Administrative Assistant offers the glue for our team. She greets team members dragging in and out of the office at the end of a long day, never forgets to circulate birthday cards for all of us to sign, and always keeps a stock of chocolate in a candy jar on her desk.

The Volunteer Coordinator and Volunteers create, innovate, and implement programs to answer patient requests—no matter how unusual. Our Volunteers Coordinator and Volunterrs are exceptional. They are generous and endless givers of their time. They offer haircuts and manicures. They weed gardens, write letters for patients, make calls on their behalf and construct a family album or memory book. They read to patients. They discuss sports while spending a couple hours watching a game with a lonely patient. Volunteers with business backgrounds help patients organize personal files, others plan a "staycation" for patients and families who can't go away on vacation, celebrate Christmas in July (or any other month if December isn't an option). They help patients visit with a loved one through Skype. One Volunteer decorator offers to paint patients' rooms a cheerful color. Once, we had a Volunteer who worked with the patient taping tags on all her furniture, art work, linens, and glassware so that family members would know which person would receive her possessions.

The Sales Team educates Doctors, Nurses, Social Workers, Discharge Planners, Case Managers, and families about Hospice and how to make a referral to a program of care. All day long, they drive to appointments at medical offices, hospitals, nursing homes, retirement homes, dialysis centers, wound care centers, and insurance companies.

A program can't survive without a great Medical Director. Once or twice a week, depending on the volume of patients on service, we meet as an Interdisciplinary Team. Patients are reviewed, the doctor adjusts orders as necessary, and the team carries out those directions. Many times the doctor will make a home visit to further assess the patient. His or her parting words at every meeting are, "Call me if you need anything." And they mean it. Patients on Hospice don't just need new medications between 8 a.m. and 5 p.m. Medical Directors are used to 3 a.m. calls from the on-call team.

Executive Directors juggle all the daily events of managing a program and stay "survey ready" at all times. Directors require a business mind, broad shoulders, and compassionate hearts, in order to manage a big family of staff and patients. We know that life is fragile and that at any time anyone can find themselves in a bed rather than beside a bed. Most of us have walked in the shoes of these families, so when we say, "We know," we truly do know. Our empathy and sympathy are genuine.

Occasionally, someone will point out how emotionally stressful Hospice work must be. I am frequently asked, "Why do you do this type of work? " I always reply, "Why not? I'm making a difference at critical times in people's lives." After difficult days, I can go home, dig in the dirt, plant flowers and herbs. Or, I can sit outside at a cafe with friends, drinking peach iced tea. I can roam through an antique store, or watch my grandchildren play a sport or dance at a recital. These activities feed my soul to go back and do it all over again. Just like every other Executive Director.

As a team, we participate in numerous walks for cures, we order Girl Scout cookies from each other's children, we discuss our favorite sitcoms, we follow local sports teams (and wear their colors on Friday). Frequently in the summer we have been known to crave DQ ice cream bars in the afternoon. In a profession where life can seem uncertain, we strive for a tone of normalcy in our office.

Recently I retired as the Executive Director but I'm back as a Volunteer. As a team, we will help make memories and learn more of life's lessons, especially the importance of time.

From the cookie jar

" The purpose of life is to live a life of purpose. "

Robert Byrne

Chapter 21

Epilogue and History of Hospice

Hospice is dedicated to providing quality end-of-life care to all patients while supporting their families throughout and after the process. "Hospice" and "hospitality" share the same root word.

Our organization considers Dame Cicely Saunders its founder and inspiration. Dame Saunders was a nurse and social worker in London before she became a physician specializing in pain control for patients suffering from advanced cancer. In 1967, she opened St Christopher's Hospice, initiating the multidisciplinary approach that we use today. In 1974, New Haven Hospice (now Connecticut Hospice) became the first Hospice in the United States. The movement has multiplied countless times. Thousands of Hospice programs serve terminally ill patients and their families throughout our nation.

One major impetus for the spread of Hospice occurred in 1982, when Medicare began offering a Hospice benefit. Patients with a life expectancy of six months who are enrolled in Medicare may sign up for Hospice, and all costs related to the terminal illness are covered. This includes four levels of care: Routine

Care, Continuous Care, Respite, and In-Patient. The Medicare benefit covers the bills for all Durable Medical Equipment (DME), including beds, wheelchairs, walkers, supplies, and all medications. Countless times I have seen such relief on a patient's face when we explain this benefit, because small Social Security checks and small pensions convince patients that it will become impossible to pay for all the equipment, medications, housing, and food they will require. The Medicare benefit provides patients with a team of professional caregivers, medical supplies, medications, pain relief, and the ability to die with dignity. Medicaid is a state-funded program that may also offer coverage for a Hospice patient.

Because Hospice team members oversee multiple cases, the patient needs a family member, friend, or other caregiver in the home to support the care plan. Patients are not required to be home-bound, however. We encourage them to take a short trip to see a grandchild graduate or to attend a wedding, if they are physically able.

Hospice programs are highly regulated, with policies and procedures. The programs of care are evaluated by state surveys.

Many insurance companies provide coverage for Hospice.

Very few Hospice patients want to stay in a hospital. When a patient chooses the option of quality care at home, the decision is cost-effective. Hospitals are sites for diagnosing, procedures, surgical procedures, emergency care, delivering new babies, and for healing. Our patients are past that point in their life cycle. As they face their end, Hospice patients need to be home, comfortable and surrounded by family members and friends who love them.

In the 1960s, Elizabeth Kubler Ross, MD, the Swiss-American psychiatrist who pioneered near-death studies and wrote the now-classic *On Death and Dying*, identified five stages of grief: denial, then anger, bargaining, depression, and acceptance. However, she also stressed that not every patient or family member goes through all five stages, and individuals may not experience them in that order.

We know that fear, especially fear of the unknown, is a destructive emotion. It can tear patients and families apart. Hospice teams strive to avoid the consequences of fear by listening and offering support on many levels and from many people.

I would like to say a deep and heart-felt thank you to every Family Member, Neighbor, Friend, Co-worker, Doctor, Nurse, Home Health Aide, Social Worker, Chaplain, Bereavement Coordinator, Volunteer Coordinator, Volunteer, Dietician, Therapist and Executive Director who is striving to provide quality end-of-life care to those in need.

From the cookie jar

"Always be a little kinder than necessary."